PI NG!

At last, the evil syndicate Team Galactic arrives
on the scene! Did something happen in the past
between Mitsumi and Team Galactic?! And now
the Pokémon battles are even more intense.
Let's all fight alongside Hareta and the others!
I'll fight too!

– *Shigekatsu Ihara*

Shigekatsu Ihara's other manga titles include
*Pokémon: Lucario and the Mystery of Mew,
Pokémon Emerald Challenge!!
Battle Frontier,* and *Dual Jack!!*.

Pokémon DIAMOND AND PEARL ADVENTURE!

Vol. 2
Perfect Square Edition

Story & Art by SHIGEKATSU IHARA

© 2008 The Pokémon Company International.
© 1995–2008 Nintendo / Creatures Inc. / GAME FREAK inc.
TM, ®, and character names are trademarks of Nintendo.
© 2007 Shigekatsu IHARA/Shogakukan
All rights reserved.
Original Japanese edition
"Pokémon D∙P POCKET MONSTERS DIAMOND PEARL MONOGATARI"
published by SHOGAKUKAN Inc.

Translation/Kaori Inoue
Touch-up Art & Lettering/Rina Mapa
Graphics & Cover Design/Hitomi Yokoyama Ross
Editor/Leyla Aker

Printed in the U.S.A.

Published by VIZ Media, LLC
P.O. Box 77010
San Francisco, CA 94107

11
First printing, September 2008
Eleventh printing, September 2018

CYRUS

A MAN WITH AN UNKNOWN PAST, HE SAYS HE'S MITSUMI'S FRIEND, BUT...

RILEY

A MYSTERIOUS YOUNG MAN WITH A LUCARIO

TEAM GALACTIC

AN EVIL ORGANIZA-TION THAT SEEKS TO EXPLOIT POKÉMON.

◀ **JUPITER**
▼ **SATURN**

BYRON

GYM LEADER OF CANALAVE CITY. DRIVES HIS TRAINERS VERY HARD.

THE STORY SO FAR

After Professor Rowan sees Hareta's innate ability to connect on a heart-to-heart level with Pokémon, he sends Hareta off with Mitsumi on a quest to find Dialga, the Pokémon that rules time. On their journey, Hareta and his partner Piplup become stronger every day—while ruining Team Galactic's schemes and getting into plenty of Pokémon battles on the way!!

CONTENTS

CHAPTER 1

BEAUTY CONTEST:

THE POKÉMON SUPER CONTEST!!

SLUMP

WE FINALLY MADE IT. HEART-HOME CITY...

DASH

HARETA!

WHAT'S THAT? LET'S CHECK IT OUT!

BOOM BOOM

HUH?

HARETA, LET'S REST A BIT...

THIS BUILDING IS HUUUGE!

9

WHOA!

HARETA, ARE YOU OKAY?!

TH-THANKS...

TM

Y-YOU'RE...!

TMP...

HAHAHA... SO YOU REMEMBERED!

STAR!

HUH? I'VE SEEN THIS STARAVIA BEFORE...

14

HERE ARE TODAY'S FOUR CONTESTANTS!!

AND OUR THREE JUDGES!

BACKSTAGE

NOW, ON TO OUR FIRST SEGMENT: THE VISUAL COMPETITION!

PIP!!!

STEAMPIPE

TA DAA

TERRIBLE...

SILENCE

NOW IT'S MY TURN TO SHOW THEM MY STYLE AND TAKE THE LEAD!

JUST AS I THOUGHT, HARETA'S OUT...

DON'T MIND THEM.

PIP...

DOOM

PIPLUP SEEMS DISCOURAGED BY THE CHILLY AUDIENCE RECEPTION!

18

WHAT?! DO THEY NOT UNDERSTAND MY ART?!

SO NOT ART!

ANOTHER CHILLY RESPONSE FOR MR. JUN!!

THEY SAY WE HAVE TO DANCE IN RHYTHM TO THIS!

KLIK KLIK

THE COMPETITORS WILL ALL DANCE TOGETHER TO THE RHYTHM!

NOW WE MOVE ON TO THE DANCE COMPETITION— AND WE HOPE TO SEE SOME FANCY DANCING!

START THE MUSIC!

OKAY! WE SHOULD BE GOOD WITH DANCING. LET'S DO THIS, PIPLUP!

PIP!

WE SURE DID DANCE A LOT BACK IN THE FOREST.

PIIIP!!

JAB

HEEEY!

PIP PIP!

YO YO!

AHAHAHAHA

THIS CONTESTANT ALSO DRAWS THE LAUGHS WITH ITS LAME MOVES!

TIP TOE

THIS IS DANCE ARTISTRY!

HAHAHAHA

NOW TO PUT THE FINAL NAIL IN THE COFFIN WITH SOME SLICK DANCING!

HE'S A LAUGHING-STOCK. IT'S OVER.

HAHAHAHA

THEY'RE BOTH AWFUL...

LOOK AT THE SMILES PASTED ON THE JUDGES' FACES AS THEY WATCH THIS COMPLETELY UNCOORDINATED DANCING!

21

YES, THE DANCING IS LUDICROUS, BUT THE FACT THAT THE POKÉMON IS DOING EXACTLY WHAT THE TRAINER WANTS IS PROOF THAT IT'S VERY ATTACHED TO THE TRAINER!

NO, I DISAGREE.

JUDGE DEXTER

...TO SEE WHAT KIND OF MOVES THIS OBEDIENT POKÉMON CAN DO!!

I'M LOOKING FORWARD TO THE ACTING COMPETITION...

ALL RIGHT! I WON'T LOSE THIS TIME, JUN!!

THAT'S MY LINE, HARETA!!

HUH?

AND NOW WE'RE ON TO THE ACTING COMPETITION! PLEASE SHOW US YOUR BEST MOVES!

22

GYAAH!

BOOOOM

...A DIRECT HIT ON THE JUDGE!!!

A CATASTROPHE! THE JUDGE DIDN'T STAND A CHANCE!!

FWEEE

AH...UM...
WELL...

GRRRR

AH...

SOMETHING'S...
BEEN
BLOWN AWAY...
THAT PROBABLY
SHOULDN'T
HAVE...

YOU TWO ARE DIS- QUALI- FIED !!!

GET OUT !!!

FIRST, MACH PUNCH!!

WHAM WHAM WHAM

WHAT INCREDIBLE SPEED!!

JAB JAB JAB JAB JAB

APE, APE, APE!!

OOPS, WENT A LITTLE OVERBOARD ON THAT ONE, HEEHEE. ♡

MY BAD...

THE DOME...

HAS ACTUALLY BEEN BURNED...

HAHAHA... YES, SHE REALLY IS SOMETHING.

THAT'S AMAZING, MITSUMI!!

THAT WAS SO COOL!!

YAAY

MM-HM, I DO KNOW HER.

HEY, YOU KNOW MITSUMI?

40

SNAP

CHAPTER 2
DIALGA'S SECRET KEYS

THE POKÉMON BATTLES ARE JUST TOO MUCH FUN! RIGHT, PIPLUP?

PIP.

GOOD JOB, HARETA! YOU HAVE FIVE BADGES ALREADY!

YEAH! I FEEL GREAT!!

I GUESS I'LL SEE YA, HARETA. I'M GOING THIS WAY!

PLUS, JUN IS OUT THERE TOO, WORKING HARD, SO I HAVE TO DO THE SAME!

YOU BETTER NOT LOSE UNTIL YOU BATTLE AGAINST ME!

IT'S A PACT!!

I'M GOING TO TRAIN HARD AND UP MY POWER!

YEAH! ME TOO!

I'M GOING TO KEEP BATTLING. I WON'T LOSE!

SMOOCH♡

WE DON'T HAVE TO DO IT RIGHT NOW, DO WE?

HUH?!

YOU WANT TO BATTLE ME? YOU'RE STRONG, AREN'T YOU?

HEY— I KNOW, MITSUMI!

MUST MOVE UNNOTICED...

MMBL MUMBLE

HAVEN'T I SEEN THAT BUTT BEFORE...?

AND THE MUTTER ING...

HEY, IT'S THAT GUY.

JIGGLE

MMBL

I MUST HURRY...

MUMBLE

RIGHT NOW THE IMPORTANT THING IS TO GET TO THE NEXT CITY...

DELIVER THE SECRET ITEM, THEN...

MUMBLE MMBL

48

50

SLICE

PIP...

GAR-
CHOMP'S
SLASH.

OR
WAS MY
HELP NOT
NEEDED?

THAT
WAS
FAST!

EVEN I
COULDN'T
SEE IT!

HEY!
THANKS
A BUNCH,
LADY!

YOU'RE
WEL-
COME ♡.

54

I WONDER IF THEY'RE PLANNING ON CAPTURING DIALGA WITH WHATEVER'S IN THAT SUITCASE?

I'LL FIND DIALGA BEFORE THEM, FOR SURE!

PAP

BUT IT LOOKS LIKE HE GOT AWAY...

AH!!

I'M ACTUALLY RESEARCHING LEGENDS.

OH, ARE YOU LOOKING FOR THE LEGENDARY POKÉMON TOO?

IN CELESTIC TOWN, JUST A BIT FARTHER FROM HERE...

...THERE'S A RELIC SITE RELATED TO THE LEGEND. I'M SURE YOU'LL FIND A CLUE THERE!

MY NAME IS CYNTHIA. NICE TO MEET YOU♡.

HEH HEH

YOU TOO, LADY?

IF YOU'RE SEARCHING FOR DIALGA, THERE'S A GOOD SPOT FOR THAT.

THE ELDER OF CELESTIC TOWN IS MY GRAND-MOTHER. COULD YOU GIVE THIS TO HER?

I'D APPRE-CIATE IT.

FWP

WELL THEN, IF YOU'RE GOING I HAVE A LITTLE FAVOR TO ASK...

OKAY! WE'RE OFF TO CELESTIC TOWN!!

SURE. I'LL BE LOOKING FORWARD TO BATTLING YOU.

MS. CYNTHIA, BATTLE AGAINST ME NEXT TIME, OKAY?!

NO PROBLEM! WE'RE OFF, THEN!

AND...

...I'D LIKE TO BATTLE AGAINST YOU AS WELL...

ARE YOU SURE?

UM, NO...

MY INTUITION TELLS ME YOU MIGHT BE A REAL CONTENDER... OR AM I WRONG?

I'M NOT VERY STRONG, SO THAT'S OKAY...

...

HARETA! YOU'RE ALREADY WAY OVER THERE?!

HEY, MITSUMI! HURRY UP!!

SO IT'S "MITSUMI," HMM...?

ANYWAY, THANKS FOR THE INFORMATION.

SO THIS IS CELESTIC TOWN!

AH! HARETA!

DASH

OKAY, LET'S GO!!

ZSH

58

OHH!!

THERE MIGHT BE MORE!!

DASH

THIS IMAGE LOOKS A LOT LIKE THE STATUE WE SAW BEFORE...

COOL! TOTALLY COOL!!

I HAVE NOTHING TO SAY TO YOU LOT!!

GET OUT!!

LEAVE CELESTIC TOWN IMMEDIATELY!!

I'M AFRAID WE CAN'T DO THAT. NOT UNTIL YOU TELL ME THE SECRETS OF THIS CAVE!!

TOK

WHAT?! WHY ARE YOU HERE?!

HEY, YOU!!

60

61

THERE ARE MURALS PAINTED HERE ABOUT THE AGE OF LEGENDS...

THE SECRETS OF POKÉMON WITH GOD-LIKE POWERS ARE SAID TO BE INSCRIBED HERE!

THE SECRET OF DIALGA... HERE?

YOU OLD HAG... MAKE FUN OF TEAM GALACTIC, WILL YOU?

RUMMAGE

WHAT?!

TWITCH

BUT I'M NEVER TELLING YOU LOT!

NYAH

JAB

62

WHA?!!

UM...

NOW WE ONLY HAVE THIRTY SECONDS LEFT!

POINK

0:30

NOW THE RELICS ARE DOOMED!

AND SO...

WHACK WHACK

BAD! BAD!

MUAHAHAHA! IT HAS A MECHANISM IN IT THAT SPEEDS UP THE TIME IF IT'S MESSED WITH!!

OW OW

PIPLUP, WE DID IT!

S-SAFE...

HOHOHO! YOU DID A GOOD JOB PROTECTING US.

AS THE ELDER, I THANK YOU.

NEVER MIND THAT—TELL ME ABOUT THE RELICS, GRANDMA!

ALL RIGHT. SINCE YOU'RE SUCH A GOOD BOY, I'LL TELL YOU AS MUCH AS YOU WANT.

OH YEAH, THIS IS FROM MS. CYNTHIA!

WHY, THANK YOU FOR DOING THIS!

AH! SO YOU'RE ONE OF CYNTHIA'S FRIENDS!

73

HARETA ...

MITSUMI, YOU'RE FRIENDS WITH THIS GUY, RIGHT?

HEY! YOU'RE THE GUY FROM BEFORE!

I WOULD NEVER BE FRIENDS WITH HIM, EVEN BY MISTAKE...

THIS MAN IS THE BOSS OF TEAM GALACTIC ...

CYRUS.

KINDA SAD THAT I'M ONLY IN ONE PANEL ...

TEAM GALACTIC'S CONSPIRACY, REVEALED!!

DON'T TRY TO ACT SO TOUGH, MITSUMI.

HOW DARE YOU TALK LIKE THAT TO MASTER CYRUS—!

JUST STANDING IN FRONT OF HIM I FEEL THIS MUCH PRESSURE!!

NH...!

YOU'RE SHAKING ALL OVER.

GRIP

?!

HEY! YOU!

THEN AGAIN, HIS POWER IS A WORLD APART FROM THE REST OF TEAM GALACTIC!

81

CLENCH....

TIME!

THERE IS ONLY ONE THING THAT I DESIRE...

THE ONE THING THAT, FOR ALL MY ENORMOUS POWER, I CAN'T DO ANYTHING ABOUT...

SHP...

THE THING THAT I AM AFTER IS THE POWER OF TIME THAT DIALGA POSSESSES.

THE POWER TO CONTROL TIME... THAT IS THE POWER OF THE GODS.

TIME IS HANDED OUT EQUALLY TO EVERYONE.

KRIK

DO YOU UNDERSTAND? I DON'T WANT TO MEET A GOD...

...AND ME, JUPITER!

WITH ME, SATURN...

SORRY, BUT BEFORE YOU GO, WHY DON'T YOU PLAY WITH US A BIT?

HARETA, GO ON.

PIPLUP, GO!!

OKAY, YOU'RE ON!

BAM

YOU GO AFTER CYRUS!

LEAVE THEM TO ME.

MITSUMI!

RIGHT! THANKS, MITSUMI!

DA SH

THAT'S RIGHT.

I'M SAYING THAT I'M MORE THAN ENOUGH TO HANDLE SOMEONE AT YOUR LEVEL.

DON'T MAKE US LAUGH!

YOU WANT TO TAKE US ON EVEN THOUGH YOU WERE SHAKING IN YOUR BOOTS JUST NOW?

THAT'S OKAY...

I'LL HELP!

BACK UP A LITTLE.

SHOULDN'T YOU BE THE ONES TO NOT TAKE ME SO LIGHTLY?

MORE THAN ENOUGH?!

DON'T TAKE US SO LIGHTLY!

SPLASH

FWOO

PIPLUP!!

BUT, TO MAKE ME BREAK A SWEAT IN BATTLE...

TO JUMP IN AFTER... THE FOOL...

HM?

THE BOY HAD POTENTIAL.

RMBL!
RMBL!

PIPLUP'S
SURF
!!!

YOU MIGHT BE A BAD GUY WHO DOES REALLY ROTTEN THINGS BUT...

...THIS BATTLE IS SUPER FUN! YOU'RE REALLY GOOD!!

HOW'S THAT, HUH?!

LET'S KEEP GOING!!

IT'S A FEELING THAT I'D LONG FORGOTTEN...

YAH!

HEH... FUN, IS IT...?

HAVE FUN IN BATTLE?! HOW COULD I, OF ALL PEOPLE, BE SWEPT UP BY AN OPPONENT?!

GET REAL!!

...MUST BE DESTROYED!!

GYA-RADOS!!

HE'S DANGEROUS!!

HARETA, HE'S MAKING ME THINK THIS WAY...

!

IT ENDS HERE.

ANYONE WHO CAN DERAIL MY PLANS...

SHP

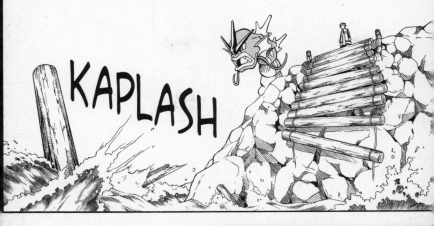

KAPLASH

BUT... THIS IS FOR THE BEST.

HOW COULD I HAVE LOST IT LIKE THAT...?

HUFF

HUFF

...FOR THE SAKE OF THE NEW WORLD.

ERASE EVERYTHING THAT GETS IN THE WAY...

FOR THE SAKE OF BECOMING A GOD!

FLEX

CHAPTER 4

CHALLENGE! THE FORTRESS OF STEEL!!

TCH...

THEY'RE RIGHT...

ARE YOU SERIOUS?

DON'T MINCE YOUR WORDS, DO YOU?

WE CAN'T WIN THE WAY WE ARE NOW...

FWAP...

HMPH.

WE MUST FIND THE THREE KEYS BEFORE THEY DO!

WE MUST NOT HAND DIALGA OVER TO TEAM GALACTIC!

SO, IN THEIR HUNT FOR DIALGA THEY'RE GOING TO CAPTURE THE THREE LEGENDARY POKÉMON...

GRRRR

COULD HE BE ANOTHER BAD GUY FROM TEAM GALACTIC...?

HOW LONG DOES A YOUNG'UN LIKE YOU NEED TO SLEEP, ANYWAY? GET UP!

WH-WHO THE HECK ARE YOU?!

HM, LOOKS LIKE YOU'RE UP NOW. IF YOU'RE AWAKE, THEN...

LET'S EAT!!!

WH

AM

WHOA! YOU'RE A GOOD GUY!!!

THIS IS THE PORT CITY OF CANALAVE.

HARETA, COME WITH ME!

HEY, WAIT!

HARETA, THIS WAY.

WOW! A SHIP! WOW!

?!

GLARE

WHERE'D HE GO?

HEY, MISTER!

TM TM TM....

THE FORTRESS OF STEEL !!!

BEHOLD, HARETA! THIS IS THE CANALAVE CITY GYM...

WHOA! I NEVER KNEW THERE WAS A GYM LIKE THIS!

THIS LOOKS TOTALLY FUN!

IT TESTS THE ABILITIES OF BOTH POKÉMON *AND* TRAINER!

THIS STRUCTURE IS RIGGED WITH A VARIETY OF TRAPS TO TEST YOUR SKILLS AS A TRAINER!

DASH

HERE I COME, MISTER !!

IF YOU WANT TO BECOME STRONGER, CONQUER THE FORTRESS AND DEFEAT ME!!

NOW WALK ACROSS WHILE DODGING THE SWINGING STEEL BEAMS!!

LET YOUR GUARD DOWN AND YOU'LL GET SMACKED BY ONE OF THE BEAMS!

OKAY! LET'S GO!

PIP!!

THUD

SO HE GOT THEM TO LET THEIR GUARD DOWN BY PRETENDING TO GIVE UP, THEN TOOK THEM DOWN ALL AT ONCE!

TM P

HW

COME ON, MISTER, TIME TO BATTLE!!

BAM

YOU KEPT RUSHING FORWARD WITHOUT CONSIDERING YOUR REMAINING STRENGTH!

YOU STILL HAVE FAR TO GO.

...IS BASTIODON'S CHARGE.

HARETA! YOU MUST RE-TRAIN YOURSELF!

IF I HADN'T MADE IT STOP, IT WOULD HAVE KNOCKED YOU OVER THE EDGE.

CHAPTER 5
SERIOUS TRAINING ON IRON ISLAND!!

151

THAT WAS AMAZING! YOU HIT THOSE ROCKS WITH YOUR EYES CLOSED!

IT WAS SENSING THE ENERGY WAVES OF THE ROCKS.

TCH! I'LL LET YOU OFF FOR TODAY!

THE GANG FROM TEAM GALACTIC HAVE BEEN SLINKING AROUND THE ISLAND RECENTLY. I WASN'T SURE IT WAS NEEDED, BUT I THOUGHT I MIGHT HELP OUT.

I'M RILEY. AND THIS IS MY FRIEND LUCARIO.

WOW!

I'M HARETA. I CAME TO THIS ISLAND TO TRAIN!

COOL! WOW! WHOA!

ALL THINGS EMIT ENERGY VIBRATIONS.

RIGHT?

AND WE'RE GOING TO GET REALLY STRONG HERE, PIPLUP!

LUCARIO IS ABLE TO SENSE THEM.

156

SHINX'S BITE!!

...THIS NEXT!!

GREAT JOB! A MISDREAVUS AND SHINX TAG-TEAM PLAY!!

YEAH, SHINX!

UP TO NOW, I'VE ONLY BEEN DEFEATING POKÉMON, BUT THIS TIME'LL BE A LITTLE DIFFERENT!

WOBBLE

BZA...P!

A TRULY PROMISING TRAINER!

EVEN IN A TOUGH SITUATION, HE BATTLES BY HELPING HIS POKÉMONS' ABILITIES SHINE!

YEAH! ONIX, I GOT YOU!!

AH! THE EGG'S MOVING!

IT'S HATCHING ALREADY?!

QUIVER

TA...DA

OH...

SMACK

JUST LIKE ME, IT'S STILL IN TRAINING!

RIOLU WANTS TO BECOME STRONG AND THAT'S WHY IT RUSHED IN.

RIO.

SHINX?

IF YOU'RE DETERMINED TO BECOME STRONG, YOU WILL!!

HAHAHA! IT'S ENERGETIC BUT A BIT TIMID, NO?

166

LUCARIO
!!

ITS HEAD IS ABLE TO SWIVEL 180°— DRAPION HAS NO BLIND SPOT!

FIRE FANG !!

RIOLU!

DASH...

HAHAHA! DRAPION IS INVINCIBLE!

THUD

THAT'S WHAT YOU GET FOR DEFYING US WHEN YOU'RE SO WEAK!

IT'S FLINCHING FROM THE BITE!

GIVE UP! YOU HAVE NO CHANCE OF WINNING!

QUIVER

QUIVER

LOOK! IT'S SO TERRIFIED THAT IT'S TREMBLING !!

KH ...!

THAT ONE CAN'T FIGHT ANYMORE! IT'S USELESS!!

YOU'RE RIGHT...I CAN SENSE WHAT RIOLU IS FEELING.

THAT'S RIGHT! SEE? WHY DON'T YOU JUST GIVE UP, AND—

BUT...

I CAN TRULY SENSE FEELINGS OF FEAR AND PAIN.

FEELINGS FOR ITS FRIENDS, THE FEELING OF NOT BEING ABLE TO FORGIVE BAD DEEDS.

CLENCH

...I CAN SENSE OTHER FEELINGS THAT ARE EVEN STRONGER.

...RIOLU WILL NEVER RUN AWAY!

EVEN THOUGH IT'S SCARED AND IN PAIN...

GR.. WHY, YOU ...

IMPOSSIBLE... DRAPION ...!

GAAHH!!

JAB

Y-YOU'D BETTER WATCH OUT!

JIGGLE

SO SHINX WAS ALL RIGHT!

?!

OKAY! ALL CLEAR, SHINX!

TA DA

TWIK

SHINX, WHAT'S THE MATTER?!

FLASH

?!

EVEN DURING A BATTLE AGAINST A POWERFUL OPPONENT LIKE DRAPION, HE WAS THINKING THAT FAR AHEAD...

HE'S PROGRESSED AT AN INCREDIBLE RATE IN SUCH A SHORT PERIOD OF TIME!

I HAD SHINX PRETEND TO BE BEATEN SO WE COULD BRING OUT RIOLU'S POWERS.

GLOOW

THIS LIGHT... COULD IT BE?!

SHINX EVOLVED INTO LUXIO!!

EVOLU-TION!!

SO YOU'VE PROGRESSED ENOUGH TO BATTLE ME, EH?

HAHAHA! LOOKING GOOD, HARETA...

RMBL

RMBL

RMBL

RMBL

RMBL

HUH?

WHAT?

GOOD! GET ON THE BOAT, HARETA!

To Be Continued in Volume 3

WHEN IS IT MY TURN AGAIN?

D·P SNAPSHOTS

PLEASE STOP CRYING!

PLANTING SEEDS

MITSUMI SOWS.

PIPLUP REAPS.

SLEEP TIGHT.

WAKE UP!

187

PIPLUP IN FLIGHT!

ACTUALLY...

In the Next Volume

Cyrus, the brilliant and ruthless leader of Team Galactic, has set in motion his grand scheme to capture Dialga. Will his nefarious plans succeed? Not if Hareta has anything to say about it! And in his battle against Team Galactic he gains a major ally when he befriends a mysterious and amazing new Pokémon.